Prayers of
HILDEGARD
of BINGEN

Walburga Storch, O.S.B., EDITOR

Introduction by Caecilia Bonn, O.S.B.
Translated by Sharon Therese Nemeth

ST. ANTHONY MESSENGER PRESS
Cincinnati, Ohio

This book is translated from the German edition
  published by Der Matthias-Grünewald-Verlag.
Copyright ©1998, Matthias-Grünewald-Verlag, Mainz

Cover icon by Robert Lentz, copyright ©1997 Robert Lentz
Cover and book design by Mary Alfieri

ISBN 0-87160-491-3

Contents

GODLY LIFE

MARY

THE CHURCH

THE WAY AND AIM OF LOVE

Foreword

Whoever searches for buried treasure or an underground water vein often has to dig deep to uncover it. But what is deeper than the human heart? A psalm verse from the *Nova Vulgata* tells us: *"Profunditas est homo et cor eius abyssus"* ("The human is extremely deep and the heart an abyss"). And what if it should be the heart of a great saint?

Then you are given Hildegard of Bingen, a multitalented personality, indeed several centuries ago described as a "miracle of the twelfth century in knowledge and holiness." We know her as a wise teacher of religious life, motherly abbess, prophetess and spiritual guide to God and eternal life for her contemporaries and beyond, up to our own time. But also her expertise as a passionate natural scientist, doctor of medicine and therapist are valued more highly today than ever before.

The visionary Hildegard was well versed in all human suffering and at the same time initiated in the secrets of God. The God-given gifts of nature and transcendence find expression in her writings, whose riches are continually being uncovered in a more extensive and deeper way. Hildegard's first work, *Scivias* (*Know the Ways*) presents what can be considered a dogma in images. *Liber Vitae Meritorum* (*Book of Life's Merits*) could be called the moralistic work of the saint. And the last of the great theological works, the *Liber Divinorum Operum* (*Book of Divine Works*) is, as it were, a natural science philosophy.

From this trilogy of Hildegard's great visionary works dealing with God, humans and the cosmos, I have compiled the simple, unpretentious, consoling words of the prayer of the saint whose visions translated into words flow from her heart and quill "in the shadow of the living light." To complete this collection I have included a range of the "sung prayers" of Hildegard, the "zither of the Holy Spirit." The poetic beauty and expressive power of these prayers form high points in the individual thematic areas in which they are grouped. The song and festival performances, often composed at the request of one of her renowned correspondents for special occasions, also contain such precious pearls from her treasury of prayer.

May this book of prayers by our great patron encourage and inspire the people of our day to let their hearts speak to God in all situations, in worship and praise, in petition and repentance, and with an unshakeable trust in his mercy.

The Benedictine Abbey of St. Hildegard
Rüdesheim/Eibingen, Germany

In the year of the 900th anniversary of
Hildegard of Bingen's birth, 1998

Sister Walburga Storch, o.s.b.

ABBREVIATIONS USED

Scivias	*Know the Ways* (Three parts with six, seven and thirteen visions respectively)
LDO	*Liber Divinorum Operum* (*Book of Divine Works*)
LVM	*Liber Vitae Meritorum* (*Book of Life's Merits*)

Excerpts from the works of Hildegard of Bingen are translations of the sources cited on page 137. Translations are by Sharon Therese Nemeth.

Introduction

The World of Thought in the Prayers of Hildegard of Bingen

When we speak to God we show our real selves in the deepest and most absolute way. Here we let down our facades and can simply express ourselves as we are. For this reason, we often turn to the words of prayer articulated by great saints. We find their inner selves in their words and encounter the very hearts of these people. The prayers of the saints can also be a help to people today who often face an overwhelming sense of wordlessness. The saints give us encouragement to overcome the lack of words we feel in our hearts and can show us how to find ourselves along our pilgrim path.

Hildegard of Bingen (1098–1179) did not leave us a prayer book in the usual sense of the word. To this extent she distinguishes herself from the great women of the Cistercian order: Saint Gertrude the Great, Mechtildis of Magdeburg and Mechtildis of Hackeborn, who just a half century later played a key role in the great blossoming of mystics in the Middle Ages.

Hildegard, who often described herself as a "trumpet of God,"[1] is first and foremost a prophet, a calling which she herself sensed as a burden weighing upon her shoulders. God does not reveal himself to her to draw her up into a mystical union, but rather calls her to go forth to the listening human race.

Therefore, while at the beginning of each of her visions the very personal "I" is used, this "I" serves as a door through which God enters. Hildegard is called to the service of making God's salvation known, which, at the very center of the Godly plan, is aimed at and embraces all of humanity and all of creation.

Dialogue between God and Humankind

The mystical writings of Hildegard, from which the prayers, songs and texts in this collection are taken, do not involve an exclusive dialogue between God and the soul. Instead, a person is addressed who is the embodiment of all that has been created, and by nature of a corporeal existence, is bound intrinsically with all of creation. The position of people in this Godly plan can be imagined as at an intersection point between vertical and horizontal planes. In this central place we are obligated not only to carry on the dialogue begun by God but also to conduct it responsibly with all creation. To realize truly our intrinsic humanness, we must—in the words of the Rhineland prophet—give ourselves up to the flow of this all-inclusive discourse. In Hildegard's words, "Let us therefore carry on a dialogue with one another." This means we are invited to enter into prayer. Prayer thus becomes a dialogue on all levels: between the Creator and the created, between one person and another, between the individual and nature, between the body and the soul, between virtue and vice.

The perpetually new and never exhausted topic of this discourse is love. The dialogue between God and human beings springs forth from the love of the Creator for his created, and likewise from the created for the Creator. "This is why the complete obedience of the created is ultimately an expression of longing for the kiss of the Creator, who gave the world everything it needed."

At the same time, God shows himself to those who faithfully look to him as if "through a window." We need this looking up and through the transcendental if we want to understand the signs of creation and our own existence in the right way and interpret their meaning. Faith, for Hildegard, means doing away with the separation between earthly and heavenly. "Every creature has visible and invisible components. The visible is weak and the invisible strong and vital." Every part of this life on earth belongs to a part of the hereafter. Faith breaks open the wall of a world that is closed into and unto itself, and opens up the window into the Godly realm. Therefore, to pray means to remain at the window of faith looking, listening, answering and acting in a responsible way.

The prayers of Saint Hildegard collected here were not expressly composed and written as such, but came about through the flow of her vision. Because of this the larger context from which the prayers were taken cannot be seen. However, it is hoped that these prayers can help us today especially, in light of our often feeling dumbstruck in the face of heaven, for devoid of any "pious wordiness," Hildegard's prayers will open the hidden wellspring in our hearts.

Wonder, Praise and Worship

Twenty-six selections have been chosen here from the seventy-six works of sacred song composed by the "Rhineland prophet."

They distinguish themselves as works artistically composed and set to music by Hildegard for use in the liturgy. Those who are familiar with the dynamic and emotional music of these hymns sense the prevailing presence of the Gothic style. These texts, born as well from the fire of Hildegard's vision, are rarely bound to rhyme and meter. They are an expression of wonder, praise and worship. The vision intensifies in them and the experience of the "Confidant of God" with the world and God becomes transparent.

To give the reader help in sorting out and more fully understanding Hildegard's language of prayer, several areas of emphasis in Hildegardian spirituality will now be examined.

The Mystery of the Beginning

In Hildegard's early work there is little hint of the Heart of Jesus passion-mystic then developing. Hildegard's vision is directed toward the heart of the Father and Creator, who reveals himself to her as "the shining One on the throne." The "utmost goodness of the Father" is the focal point of all dramatic events that take place between God, people and the world. This is our birthplace, our one true home. Like a small, heart-shaped lump of clay, we rest in the heart of the Father, who lovingly cleans, cares for and adorns us. Out of the heart of our Creator we are placed into existence with an embrace and a kiss. Because of our origin from this "mystery of the beginning," every person senses an "innate longing for the embrace and kiss, without which we would wither." In the depths of our heart we will never lose the memory of our origin, which is at the same time our final destination. For in his highest goodness expressed in the act of creation, God has become our Mother. Likewise, the incarnated Christ became our Brother by receiving what also nourishes us at the "maternal bosom" of the Father. Therefore, nothing is "sweeter" than to hasten to the Creator of the universe because, "I want to

follow you because you are my Creator."
The created knows what it is to have been
born of and touched by the Father.

And so we may see God, recognize,
touch, savor him and rest in his lap. Those
who pray with the words of Saint Hildegard
are therefore aware of their innate dignity
as the created. While through our own
means we do not have the capability for
goodness, when we turn to God in prayer
all of the Lord's creative power is at our
disposal. Hildegard sees what is reserved
for angels, who witness face to face how
the heart of the Father breathes out his inner power: a godly dynamic (*virtutes*),
which sustains, heals and wards off all
that is deadly and chaotic. This power is
transformed as strength-giving virtue in
people, giving them the ability for their
mission in the world. Thus, people work
together with God, indeed even becoming,
in a sense, creators themselves. In prayer-
ful appeal to the Creator, the created finds
the way to the self, secure in the knowledge of being adequately fortified for this

journey. It seems almost like a definition of what it means to be human when Hildegard writes, "The created one is like a cry, a scream, a voice. O how pitiable and at the same time wonderful is this voice, for God sets such fragile vessels with all his miracles among the stars."

The Misery of Humanity

Face to face with God we not only recognize our dignity but also, with deep anguish, the abysmal misery of our brokenness because "we have forgotten our Creator." Hildegard acknowledges, "I am like ash and cinders in the ground of my soul and dust in the wind. I am not worthy of being called human. Great is my fear." Similarly, in advanced years she directs the request to her secretary, Guibert of Grembloux, "Pray that I do not fall, because even Peter did not remain steadfast."

When we sin we experience ourselves as strangers, driven into exile, homeless and deprived of all happiness, as if we were imprisoned and bound in chains. In sinning we have not only trespassed against our Lord but also alienated ourselves from God's creation inherent in our existence, thereby blotting out our own faces. This misery of the descent into sin, rooted in forgetting God and the accompanying slide into indifference, is expressed in the prayers of Saint Hildegard in an abundance of images: "I look at my wounds." The dignity and misery of humankind—how can we live without betraying one for the other, or being constantly torn between these two poles, not only as sinners but as the righteous as well? How can we master the art of living a Christian life and unite these extremes? In view of these questions, Hildegard strikes the most beautiful and compelling chord of her spirituality when she speaks of the all-empowering force of repentance. Her works are imbued with the image of the prodigal son returning home to his father. The idea of repentance and the "groaning of the soul" are recurring themes in the prayers as well and, as such, need to be addressed in more detail.

The Healing Power of Repentance

For Hildegard, the "shining One on the throne" is constantly at work transforming the dirty clay, the festering wounds and broken limbs of the sinner into pearls and precious jewels. He immerses these in the light of his utmost goodness by the power of the blood of the Son, who wants to carry back to his Father the one who has been wounded. However, this cannot take place without our direct involvement. It is an event which moves heaven and earth, Hildegard tells us, when the one who has gone astray remembers the Creator, and looking up to him begins to speak, "I want to set out and return to my Father." Before turning back it is essential that we fix our eyes on our wounds and no longer hide or deny them. "I seek the wounds of your heart," says the Son of Man, "show me the wounds of your heart." The Son of God

answers the revelation of our wounds by
revealing his own, saying, "I want to suffer
with you in your wounds and in doing so
give you communion with the Father."

It is, in fact, the sinner who takes the
decisive step through the power of grace. It
is a turning away from the self when the
sinner eagerly arises, as if from a deep
sleep, and, filled with the driving force
of repentance, hastens back to the Father:
"For I will unconditionally receive at
once, and deliver into freedom the one
who has sinned." In the embrace of God
and the mystery of our origin we reawaken and, freed from the bonds of sin,
regain our well-being, not because we have
obtained a critical understanding of our
own shadow, but because we have set out
toward God. For Hildegard, taking this
step toward God is the most important
moment in spiritual life: "I want to be with
those who understand me through true
penance. I even wed myself with them in
the dirt of humanity, because I want to
make them pure."

Repentance is therefore the epitome of curative medicine for Hildegard, not only for the soul but also for the body. Without it, every kind of healing only treats the symptoms. Far from wanting to cover people with a cloak of guilt, repentance actually frees us from the web of fear. Repentance is not only a healing power, but the structure of the entire world order rests upon its pillars. It intervenes in the processes of life, moving and changing history and the cosmos, for with it "we touch the stars." Through repentance God brings home creation poisoned by the error of humanity.

Yearning for God:
The Groaning of the Spirit

Another term also needs to be looked at in this context, one that has completely lost its meaning for us today, yet plays an important role in Hildegard's writings, that is "the groaning of the soul." The memory of God, our home in him and the simultaneous confrontation of our wounds release a wrenching twofold pain within us incorporating the longing for God and the experience of our own helplessness. This wrenching sensation is expressed as a groan tearing us away from ourselves to God and is an important physical and spiritual process countering all repression. "Body and soul form an alliance, expressed mutually in a groan. This is heaven: to raise myself up in the righteous groan of longing. In my groaning I look to God." This is not an expression we "create" ourselves, but a source we can draw upon.

In the eighth chapter of the letter to the Romans, Saint Paul gives us a theology of the spiritual meaning of this expression. We are told that all of nature groans in the pains of labor. In the same way, humankind groans in anticipation of its salvation. When we do not know how to pray the Spirit itself intercedes for us with inexpressible groaning and, in this way, calls the Father (Romans 8:22–26). Essentially, it is God himself who compels us to this groan of longing. Hildegard thus categorically explains, "Who does not have the groaning of the spirit will not believe." This means that some will not open up fully to let God enter the spirit. In groaning we touch the heart of God like a child who throws itself onto the lap of father or mother to find comfort there after a hurtful experience.

Hildegard rejects the possible objection of being unable to give voice to this expression in spirit, explaining, "You forbid your soul crying and groaning and prevent it from seeking help by me. But how can I answer someone whose voice I never hear? You groan no more to me, and so you also ask nothing of me. Who does not groan out to me has forgotten me."

The Fragrance of Good Works

For Hildegard, repentance is the first of the so-called good works. Each time we freely make the decision to set out on the path to the home of our Creator, we are also

following the way of God's commandments "as a deer hastens to a spring." Seen
in this way the commandments are neither
strict rules nor an ascetic imperative, but
something that bring us joy and which we
can "savor." In the good works of virtue
we become God's partner.

We are empowered by the heart of our
Creator who, like a bride, offers us a loving
union whose fruit is the works of virtue.
We may then glorify God and, awakening
to our true self, play a part in the formation
of this world and the next. But we are
asked to make a decision for ourselves con-
cerning an existence that hangs between
the balance of good and evil. The way of
repentance is the only response to failing in
goodness. Everything else belongs to the
realm of death. Some of Hildegard's com-
ments to this theme can give the impres-
sion of hostility toward the body, as the
decision for goodness involves a continual
struggle against desire and weaknesses of
the flesh. Hildegard however uses the word
"flesh" in an exclusively biblical sense to

describe the godforsaken and evil tendencies of the fallen nature of humankind. She clearly makes a distinction between this and a positive spirituality of the body, which was revolutionary for her time:

> As is worthy of the Creator, you have clothed me in the purest flesh...you have lengthened the hem of your robe, girded with the belt of your praise. The soul cannot act without the body. It needs the body to express itself rightfully; indeed it is a joy for the soul to act within the body.

Thus, the body and the soul are not rivals battling against each other but born partners. Their interaction is admittedly not without conflict, but it is exactly for this reason that they both need to remain in dialogue and care for each other as lovers, so that their work comes to fruition for God. The fragrance of good works flows from the body, for as humans we are of a physical nature to our very core.

The Golden City

These twenty-six songs undoubtedly belong to the most prolific texts among Hildegard's works. In them the abundance of her words and prayer flow together expressing wonder, worship and praise. In the Golden City beyond the window, she sees the completed edifice of the utmost goodness of the Father, which the faithful in this life have been borne to as stones and set into place. The Golden City, the house of the glory of the Lord, becomes the dwelling place of the faithful, the Mother Zion to whom Hildegard calls. She yearns for the sound of the ultimate harmony of all things created, voiced in unison with the choir of angels. Therefore, we have the often-repeated "O" in her spiritual songs, and the great interval leaps in arrangement break the sober discipline and tranquil plainchant of the classic Gregorian choral. And yet the fullness of composition here also flows again into the clear objectivity of her vision.

Mary—Archetype for Creation and the Church

At the point of intersection between heaven and earth and God and humans is Mary. She is repeatedly addressed in Hildegard's songs, in which she is praised in the liturgy of the church as the "window to heaven." The nine lyrical works in this book treating Mary are among the finest pearls of Marian praise. In the canonization files of Saint Hildegard, eyewitness accounts report that the love of Mary surrounded Hildegard like a radiant light when she sang with her sisters in the cloister.

A richness of images shines through in these songs, and readers should simply let themselves be immersed in them. However, a few guidelines can help one to rediscover Mary in these songs today. Hildegard gives the figure of the Mother of God specifically cosmic characteristics. The Creator of the world "looks above all other creatures to the countenance of the most beautiful of women, as the eagle looks to the sun." A

striking image. Like looking into a mirror,
the Creator sees the undistorted, unspoiled
concept of his great plan reflected in Mary.
Thus, she becomes the "embrace of all
that has been created." Hildegard similarly
interprets the Wisdom texts of the Old
Testament in terms of Mary:

> The LORD created me at the beginning
>   of his work,
>   the first of his acts of long ago.
> Ages ago I was set up,
>   at the first, before the beginning
>   of the earth.
> When there were no depths I was
>   brought forth,
>   when there were no springs
>   abounding with water....
> When he established the heavens,
>   I was there,
>   when he drew a circle on the
>   face of the deep,...
> and I was daily his delight,
>   rejoicing before him always....
>   (Proverbs 8:22 ff.).

Mary is the dawn, the radiant substance of the sunrise, and golden fundament of the world, a presence filled and permeated by God. As the second Eve she has become the helper from the side and on the side of the Son of God. She has become the mother of the living and author of life. Hildegard's words, however, clearly distinguish themselves from any kind of sentimentality or the archaic cult of a primal mother. She describes Mary's uniqueness in terms of an unspoiled existence of archetypal purity, an existence having nothing to do with ascetic accomplishment but entirely founded on grace, for example, "Your chastity is glory from God, sacred creation."

Again and again the poet and singer's gaze turns to the body, the fruitful womb of the Virgin. The unutterable mystery and wondrous event of the Incarnation captivate Hildegard. Already on the first day of creation, God entrusted not only his only eternal Son to the womb of Mary but also his sacred work, the church.

Mary is not only the radiant, golden, primal substance of creation, but she is also the archetypal womb of all holiness, the builder of life and life-giving instrument. She shows us how grace makes the perfect fulfillment of nature possible. In a number of images the mystery of the church is similarly brought to light. Mary and the church are connected to each other, one reflected in the other. Mary is the church personified. Both of these images remain open to each other. The Mother Zion, which can be understood as both Mary and the church, is ultimately the maternal love of God.

As the completely holy one, Mary is also the mother of healing; indeed she herself is the soothing balsam for the wounds of our misery after the fall of Eve. She shows us her mercy in other ways as well. She walks with us along our path as a prophet, eternally filled with the Holy Spirit, calling to us in a never-ceasing voice time after time when we fall. Through the power of the Holy Spirit, which eternally shines upon her and graces her with fruitfulness, Mary becomes the rescuer of the entire human race. The Holy Spirit is for her the "dynamic of the universe and root of creation."

The Holy Spirit as Life-giving Power

What is the Holy Spirit of God? In two songs Hildegard gives us the answer to this question. She calls it the living one, the inner impulse and prime mover of all life. It is the "life of life." Life has a holistic meaning for Hildegard. First, it means creation in concrete terms. The life-giving spirit of God touches the entire creation in all of its processes. Everywhere we come in contact with life we can sense its power and are moved by God. "You, life of all living creatures, you breathe life into all things."

But life is also wisdom and understanding. King Solomon placed the gift of wisdom before all riches and sovereignty. "You continually beget people full of understanding, made joyful by the breath of wisdom." Through wisdom and understanding we become open and able to

receive life-giving power from the heart of
God and are commissioned to act in this
world. The Holy Spirit leads us on in this;
it flows through our actions and, in doing
so, we are able to savor it. Spiritual teach-
ers and mystics call the unutterable that
we sense when the breath of God reaches
us and draws us to love "sweetness." The
spirit of God is holy. Through it "the cosmos glows and erupts." It impels and
moves us to good works with its "fiery
power," through which we can build and
heal, through which we can conquer everything that stands in the way of life. The
Holy Spirit is pure water and a mirror in
which we are allowed to see the reflection
of God's caring love for the sinner caught
in the snares of misery. "You anoint the life-
threatening afflictions and clean the festering wounds." Here Hildegard is once again
exploring her favorite theme, repentance:

> You have raised up a new tower
> amidst the publicans and sinners, who
> confess their sins and offenses to you.
> And thus every creature praises you,

because you are the precious ointment
for the broken-hearted and the festering wounds which you transform into
precious pearls.

The holiness of the spirit of God is praised
here in the mystery of its endless mercy.
Truly the "godly power will save." The
plan of salvation is at the same time a plan
of unification or, "You, hope of all members
for unity." For the modern-day person,
however, many things have come apart.
We have fallen out of the mesh of this
godly relationship through our own actions and have even succeeded in unravel-
ing it completely. God's spirit, however,
seeks to gather together and bind in unity.
"You, mighty way, that runs through
everything...you connect and enclose all
into one." The Holy Spirit is guarantor of
human dignity and the joy of life. It is the
sound and the voice of our praise.

Consummated in Christ

Our prayer has its source and ultimate end in the dialogue of the Son of God with the Father. Before the dawn of time this unbroken dialogue, to which we are invited, existed. Our weak and hesitant discourse with heaven is carried upon it, enfolded by it and flows to this end. Thus, the moving words of the Son to the Father are rightfully placed at the conclusion of this collection, which also forms the climax of Hildegard's works, *The Book of Divine Works* and her short drama *The Play of the Virtues*. Beseechingly the Son shows the Father his wounds, which remain open as long as people on this earth continue to sin. Christ not only reveals the stigmata as a sign of his Incarnation, but it is also the deepest expression of his solidarity with us sinners, indeed with the entire languishing creation.

> Father, see my distress for the members
> of my body. The sum of their numbers
> cannot be allowed to diminish until you
> behold my body covered in gemstones.

Father, I suffer from exhaustion. Look upon my wounds! The creation that you fashioned at the beginning in the greenness of vitality cannot be allowed to wilt and wither away.

The great themes of Hildegard's vision once again come to the forefront: the fall and restoration, the healing of sinful people through suffering revealed and the salvation in becoming one with the wounds of the Lord. The prayer closes with the prophetic call to bend our knee before the Creator and Father, so that we can take the loving hand he offers us to consummate his beloved work in us.

Readers of this book are invited to open their hearts to the words of prayer of Saint Hildegard. With these words one of the greatest female figures of more than 900 years ago has left us a moving witness of living faith. This book has fulfilled its purpose when just one text opens the dialogue to God in the heart of the beholder.

Sister Caecilia Bonn, O.S.B.

Note

[1] The quoted material in this section is taken from
the writings of Saint Hildegard of Bingen.

Hildegard of Bingen—
A Portrait

by Sharon Therese Nemeth

Although she was firmly rooted in the world of the early Middle Ages, Hildegard of Bingen is a person who can serve as a role model for us today. Hildegard's choice to follow God's calling is reflected in a life lived to the fullest, sustained by trust in the divine plan of salvation, which embraces every element of creation as an integral part of the universe.

Hildegard chose early in life to express herself as an individual. This was at a time in history when women were considered second-class citizens at best, a fact which did not deter her from following a personal path marked by her faith in God. A highly

gifted, artistic person, Hildegard of Bingen
was a great prophet and mystic—the author of unparalled visionary works. She
was a diplomat, not afraid to stand up for
the truth, who gave frank counsel to the
emperors, kings and popes of her day.
Hildegard's holistic approach to life is seen
in her work as a doctor of homeopathic
medicine and healing. Her skill as a natural
scientist is as impressive today as it was in
Hildegard's lifetime. She was a composer
of music and liturgical song, and she even
invented a private language. It was also
her personal sense of integrity in acting
upon her faith in all areas of life that
touched people so deeply during her time.
Those who supported her—from the renowned, such as Pope Eugenius III and
Saint Bernhard of Clairvaux, to the name-
less, who journeyed to her cloister seeking
her help in their emotional and physical
distress—did so with confidence in the
guiding Spirit behind her great words and
deeds. Hildegard's stations in life reflect
qualities of her person that are as fresh and

genuine to us today as they were in the Middle Ages: her empathy and compassion toward others and the unwavering sense of justice and courage she displayed in the face of opposition and physical disability.

Early Life

Hildegard was born in 1098 in Bermersheim, a village southwest of Mainz in the Rhine Hessen area of Germany. She was the tenth and last child of Hildebert and Mechthild, a couple of high-ranking nobility. Two of Hildegard's brothers entered clerical life, and one of her sisters lived as a nun in Hildegard's cloister.

When Hildegard was eight years old she was placed in the care of Jutta of Spanheim, a pious young noblewoman. In all probability Hildegard first lived with Jutta at her family's residence, not far from Bermersheim, while Jutta spent time finding a suitable site for a convent. The custom of giving up children to life in a cloister, who were then called oblates (from

Latin *oblati*, meaning "offering"), was an accepted and honorable practice in the Middle Ages, particularly among wealthy families. Cloisters were dependent on the financial support received from their members in the form of a dowry or inheritance and were thus able to support and maintain their own self-sufficiency. In Hildegard's case, her role as an oblate had a special biblical significance, since she was the tenth child in her family. Hildegard stated later that she was in full agreement with her entry into religious life as an oblate, although she just as strongly objected to the practice of a person being forced into monastic life against her will (although for many this was, in fact, the preferred alternative to marriage).

Jutta and Hildegard, along with another young female religious, found their home at the Benedictine abbey of Disibodenberg in 1112. At this time Jutta was twenty years old and Hildegard fourteen. There is evidence that the young women were bound by a close friendship, a significant factor during Hildegard's formative years. The enclosed living area of the young women at the Disibodenberg monastery was initially an anchorage near the monk's main abbey. Under Jutta's guidance the anchorage soon became a convent for Benedictine nuns. Hildegard was between fourteen and seventeen when she formally joined the Benedictine order. Hildegard was a Benedictine with heart and soul and as such lived the life of a contemplative nun according to the Rule of Saint Benedict. She later took on her public role out of a sincere conviction that she must act based on her responsibility toward the church, giving witness to crucial matters of faith that were being ignored by others. This was clearly not a role she always welcomed or that came easily to her. At Disibodenberg, Hildegard learned how to read Latin and became versed in the Bible and Psalter, and also learned to play the harp as an accompaniment to liturgical prayer. It was Hildegard's lack of a formal higher education—which would, in any case, have been unthinkable for a woman of her day—which led her to characterize herself as "unlearned."

Jutta was a remarkable woman in her own right who clearly had a decisive influence on Hildegard's personal growth. Her life was focused, defined by a desire to follow the will of God. A report from Jutta's early life tells us that she took the vows of sisterhood at fourteen, despite opposition from her family. Around this time she also had the fervent wish to set out on a solitary pilgrimage. She was, however, held back from doing so by her well-intentioned brother who feared for her safety. Jutta was a wise teacher who recognized and fostered Hildegard's gifts. When Jutta died in 1136 at the age of forty-four, Hildegard was unanimously chosen by the sisters to become her successor (*magistra*) at the blossoming nuns' monastery. Hildegard's leadership of the cloister followed the example set by Jutta, and she quietly carried out her vocation for forty-three years before her life changed dramatically.

In her autobiography Hildegard writes that she had already begun to experience visions when she was three years old. It was then that the great light revealed to her first moved her soul. Understandably, these revelations created feelings of uncertainty and fear in Hildegard. She wondered initially if such visionary ability was not the norm for all people, but when her nursemaid negated her question to this effect, Hildegard sensed at once that she must keep this special gift hidden from others lest it be misconstrued. Later at Disibodenberg Hildegard's visionary gift was recognized by Jutta, who became her first confidant. From her early years Hildegard was also plagued by weak health that could manifest itself in a difficulty in walking, even paralysis, and other painful physical ailments.

A Turning Point

In the foreword to her first work, *Scivias* (*Know the Ways*), Hildegard writes of the turning point in her life when she was called to reveal her visions to the public eye. This occurred in 1141 shortly before Hildegard turned forty-three. At that time, she writes in the foreword to *Scivias*, a fiery light flowed through her brain and filled her heart like a flame. It was a light that did not burn but warmed like the sun. She was filled with a divine understanding of the psalms, the Scriptures and the holy books of the Bible, as she heard a voice from heaven instruct her, "Tell and write what you see and hear...do not write as is pleasing to you or as another thinks is right, but according to the will of the One who knows, sees, and orders all in the hidden depths of his mysterious wisdom." Hildegard emphasizes that what she saw and heard was not perceived in a dream or in a state of mental confusion, but with a clear mind while she was wide awake. Her "inner eye and ear" received the divine message in a place only God can enter.

It is not surprising that Hildegard was hesitant to follow this directive. She had kept her visions hidden for many years, only confiding what she experienced to Jutta. Furthermore, according to the interpretation of the Pauline dictates in the Middle Ages, it was forbidden for women to write, preach and hold public sermons. She knew the trials that would most likely await her if she made her visions known to the outside world. Hildegard herself attributed her hesitation to feelings related to her inability, rather than to stubbornness in following the directive from heaven. This refusal was followed by a severe period of illness, which Hildegard later saw as the consequence of her initial protest to follow God's will. In spite of her personal conflicts, Hildegard felt a responsibility toward her church and for an exegesis of the Scriptures, often neglected by the clergy of her time. Encouraged by her friend and teacher, the Disibodenberg monk Volmar, Hildegard set out upon the task of recording her visions in what became her first visionary work, *Scivias*.

Volmar had been designated to act as a prior and father confessor of the nuns' convent at Disibodenberg as the cloister grew in size. He served as Hildegard's loyal secretary, transcribing her visions in letter-perfect Latin for more than thirty years, and also became one of Hildegard's dearest friends. Additionally, Hildegard received invaluable assistance in recording her visions from Richardis of Stade, one of her sisters at the Disibodenberg cloister. Richardis was a relative of Jutta's and from what we know of her, a sensitive, gifted person. She and Hildegard also shared a close friendship.

The Synod of Trier in 1147 to 1148 was a significant turning point for Hildegard's personal calling, and what transpired there in connection with her work empowered her with an authority that cannot be underestimated. At the time of the synod, Abbot Kuno, the abbot of the Disibodenberg cloister, passed on parts of the unfinished *Scivias* to Archbishop Heinrich of Mainz. The archbishop in turn presented these sections to Pope Eugenius III at the synod. The reaction to Hildegard's visions was a thoroughly positive one. At the synod, a deeply moved pope read aloud excerpts to the cardinals and bishops present and was met with applause. Saint Bernard of Clairvaux, who was also in attendance and, in fact, knew Hildegard personally, also expressed his strong support of her work publicly, which he had previously conveyed to Hildegard in their now famous correspondence. Thus Hildegard received the necessary papal backing to make her visions public and to put them in public oral and written form. As Hildegard acted fully on this special allowance, her reputation grew and visitors streamed to the cloister. A new phase in Hildegard's life had dawned, in which her multi-faceted talents found open expression.

A New Cloister

At approximately the same time, Hildegard received a vision telling her to leave

Disibodenberg in order to found a new cloister for her nuns. In the vision Hildegard was told to settle the cloister in Rupertsberg, across from Bingen. This divine directive seems logical to us today in the circumstances. Many daughters of wealthy families had the wish to join Hildegard and her sisters, and the convent at Disibodenberg could no longer accommodate the many postulates who flocked there.

However, the plan to form a new cloister was far from an easy undertaking. Abbot Kuno and many of the monks at Disibodenberg expressed vehement opposition to this venture, even going so far as to question the directive of Hildegard's vision. The stressful situation caused a downturn in Hildegard's health, but with outside intervention permission was granted. This saving grace was due in large part to the help of Richardis of Stade, the mother of the nun at Hildegard's cloister who bore the same name. Richardis the elder contacted the archbishop of Mainz, Heinrich I, directly and received his backing for Hildegard. Thus, Abbot Kuno finally gave his approval for the move.

When Hildegard and the first twenty sisters came to the patch of arid land near Bingen in 1150 they were faced with a huge task. Hildegard had been able to purchase the land for the Rupertsberg cloister with the help of benefactors, which meant that the property was in entire possession of the abbey. But the sisters had little other financial assistance at this time and were often grateful just to have enough to eat.

The financial livelihood of the Rupertsberg cloister remained under the jurisdiction of the Disibodenberg monastery. This meant that the dowries and financial gifts the sisters had brought with them upon joining the nuns' cloister were still controlled by the Disibodenberg monastery. To make matters worse, Volmar, who was now the acting prior at Rupertsberg, was suddenly faced with the very real prospect of being called back to Disibodenberg.

The latter point was the "straw that broke the camel's back," compelling Hildegard to make a surprise visit to the Disibodenberg cloister. Hildegard did not mince words in confronting the monks she saw acting against the sisters' best interests. Finally, an agreement was reached that regulated the monetary interests of the Rupertsberg cloister. Furthermore, the nuns were granted the right to choose a prior who could not be withdrawn without their approval. These rights were guaranteed by the archbishop of Mainz, who additionally granted the Rupertsberg cloister sole jurisdiction in choosing their abbess. Much later in 1163 Hildegard obtained an additional document securing the rights of the Rupertsberg cloister from none other than Frederick Barbarossa.

In the years of resettlement to Rupertsberg, Hildegard completed work on *Scivias* (1151). There followed a prolific period of writing in which Hildegard's genius could be seen reflected in a variety of directions. Between 1151 and 1158 Hildegard enriched the liturgy with her choral musical compositions that became the work, *Symphonia*. She wrote medical and scientific treatises known as *Physica* and *Causae et curae* (*Causes and Cures*). In 1158 she began *Liber vitae meritorum* (*The Book of Life's Merits*), which would be the second in her trilogy of visionary works.

The emotional turbulence of this time was also felt by Hildegard in the tragic loss of her friend and "daughter," the nun Richardis of Stade, who had helped Hildegard so faithfully with her work. In 1151 Richardis received notice that she was to leave Rupertsberg and take on the position of abbess at the cloister Bassum in Saxony. Richardis's brother was bishop in Bremen in this province and had ordered this reassignment. Hildegard was desperate at this turn of events but unable to influence the situation despite her efforts, and, accordingly, Richardis left the Rupertsberg cloister. It is not entirely clear how Richardis herself felt about this situation, but there is evidence that she wished to return to Rupertsberg after several months at the new abbey, a wish to which her brother also consented. However, before she was able to realize this plan, Richardis suffered a serious illness and died at Bassam on October 29, 1152.

Preaching Tours

Hildegard's precarious health took a downward turn between 1158 and 1162. She suffered severe bouts of fever, breathing difficulty and exhaustion so extreme at times that her death seemed imminent. However, we also know this as the time that she embarked on her first of four preaching tours. The first tour occurred sometime after 1158 and took Hildegard to Mainz, Wertheim, Kitzingen, Ebrach and Bamberg. Hildegard's reputation had spread throughout Europe by this time, and she was brought together with the renowned figures of religion and politics, with whom she also carried on a lively written correspondence. Over 300 of her letters have been preserved and offer valuable testimony to her inner and outer nature. Hildegard's time was wrought with a decline in the morals of the clergy and the public at large, thus it was important for her to seek contact with all segments of the population. She warned of the consequences of falling away from the teachings of Christ and strove to convey awareness for the necessity of a life lived in harmony with God and all creation. Hildegard preached in churches and cloisters, as well as in market places and public squares. For a woman, this alone was unheard of in the history of the church.

Hildegard's second preaching tour took her to Trier in 1160 and to Metz and a Benedictine cloister in Kauftal in the diocese of Strasbourg. In 1163, at the same time as her third preaching tour up the Rhine River to Andernach, Cologne and Werden, Hildegard completed work on *Liber vitae meritorum* (*The Book of Life's Merits*). She also began writing her third visionary work, *Liber divinorum operum* (*The Book of Divine Works*), which was completed in 1173.

In 1165 Hildegard acquired an empty
cloister in Eibingen, next to Rüdesheim,
and founded a second abbey there. A
group of her nuns settled there and
Hildegard, the acting abbess, visited the
monastery twice a week. Hildegard set
out on her fourth preaching tour in the
Swabia area of Germany in 1170 to 1171.
Hildegard, seventy years old at this time,
traveled throughout southern Germany,
stopping at the cloister Alzey and continu-
ing on to Maulbronn, Hirsau, Kirchheim
and Zwiefalten. It was an astounding feat,
considering the difficulty of travel at this
time, either by foot or on horseback.

Courage in the Face of Challenge

At the end of Hildegard's life, she was
forced to confront a difficult turn of events,
again testing her mettle. Her reaction
to this challenge is exemplary of the
courage Hildegard expressed her entire
life. The conflict erupted in 1178 when an
excommunicated nobleman was buried on

the grounds of the Rupertsberg monastery. Hildegard was told by the Mainz episcopate that his body must be removed from the abbey grounds—but she refused to follow this order. Hildegard held to her conviction that the young man had confessed his wrongdoings and received absolution before his death, thus his burial on the hallowed grounds of the monastery was justified. But because of her refusal to exhume the body, an interdict was placed on the cloister. This meant that public church services, the sacrament of the Eucharist, as well as liturgical song, were forbidden; the nuns were allowed only to recite the psalms and readings in a muted voice. This was a terrible blow for Hildegard and her sisters, and Hildegard's hope for the intervention of the prelate of Mainz remained without result. However, Hildegard remained true to the faith which had guided her throughout life and upheld her position. Finally the intervention of Archbishop Christian of Mainz provided the catalyst for ending the interdict.

Hildegard was able to spend the last few months of her life living the sacramental life of the church that was her lifeblood, and her cloister was restored to the position where, in the spirit of Saint Benedict, God could be glorified in all things.

Hildegard of Bingen died on September 17, 1179, at the age of eighty-two. The hagiography tells of the appearance of two radiant arcs of light which met to form a cross in the sky on the night she died. There were reports of miracles following her death, and, in fact, so many pilgrims flooded the Rupertsberg Abbey that the archbishop of Mainz had to step in to preserve the contemplative life of the sisters.

Hildegard's legacy is carried on today in her life story, writings and musical compositions, as well as in countless secondary works based on her wisdom. Throughout her life and work Hildegard unwaveringly reflected her deep belief in the divine plan for humankind and its place at the heart of the cosmos, connected with all of creation in a web woven by God.

Prayers of
HILDEGARD
of BINGEN

Redeemed
Creation

Creator and Redeemer

O elemental power of eternity,
in your heart
you have ordered the universe.
You have created the universe through
    your Word,
according to your will.
And your Word became flesh
in the form
that descended from Adam.
In this way the deepest pain
was taken from our body.

Indeed, how marvelous is your goodness,
O Savior!
Through your incarnation
you have set all things free.
From the breath of God you became man
freed from the bondage of sin.
Glory to you, Father, and your Son,
with the Holy Spirit.

In this way the deepest pain
was taken from our body.

—"Song," Nr. 58

Sacred Observance

O fire of the consoling spirit,
life of life for all creatures.

You are holy for you kindle life in
    the created.
You are holy for you clean the
    festering wounds.
You are holy for you anoint the
    dangerous afflictions.
Breath of all holiness, fire of love,
    sweet essence we drink into our core,
fragrance of virtue you embed in
    our hearts.

You are a pure spring where we behold
    God as he gathers up the confused
and searches for the lost.

O defender of life, you, hope of unity
    for your members,
O girdle of upright honor, bring holiness
    to the blessed!

Protect those held captive by the enemy,
free those bound in chains;

the godly power wants to save them.
You, mighty way, that stretches across
    the breadth of all things
in the heavens, on the earth, through
    the depths,
you ordain and encircle everything
    into one.

By your power the clouds blow,
the air streams,
the stones shift,
the creeks gush into springs,
and the earth sprouts green.

For all time you have begotten people
full of understanding,
made happy through the breath of
    wisdom.

And so you shall be praised,
you, voice of laudation,
you, joy of life,
you, hope and mighty glory,
because you grant the gifts of light.

—"Song," Nr. 19

Divine Happiness

When I gaze with open eyes
at what you, my God, have created here,
heaven is already mine.

In serenity I gather into my lap
roses and lilies and everything green,
while praising your works.

I ascribe my works to you.
Joy springs from sadness,
and joy brings divine happiness.

—LVM Pitra V, 17 (XI)

Quickening Spirit

Holy Spirit,
you, quickening life,
prime mover of the universe
and root of all creation,
cleanse your creation from impurity,
heal the guilt and anoint the wounds.

O radiant life, worthy of praise,
awaken and reawaken the universe!

—"Song," Nr. 15

God's Works

I want to rejoice, O God,
protected and defended by you
I am freed from the burden of sins.
To follow in your good works is now
    the longing of my soul.
Called from the depths of my groaning,
    drawn by your power,
you have placed me in your shelter,
    safe from my enemies.

I am truly the work you have created;
before the dawn of time you willed to
    form me as I am
and to subjugate creation to me.
At that time you granted me the ability
to parallel my actions with yours.
And so I belong to you alone.

As is worthy of the Creator,
you have clothed me in the purest flesh,
you have lengthened the hem of
    your robe,
girded with the belt of your praise.
Who looks upon you with the eyes
    of faith,
God of the Trinity, will not perish.

—LDO III, 7 Migne 972D–973C (XI)

(cf. Psalm 62. Biblical citations following
prayers in this section indicate passages
commented and meditated upon by
Hildegard in the individual prayers.)

Destined for Salvation

O eternal God,
work in us through the burning embers
   of your love,
so we may become your limbs,
created in the same love
with which you begot your Son at the
   first dawn
before creation.

See the grief that has overcome us;
free us for the sake of your Son
and lead us to the joy of salvation.

—"Song," Nr. 2

Abandonment
and Doubt

Doubt

O God, have you not created me?
The wretchedness of earth presses
    down upon me!
And so I must flee and hide myself
    from you like Adam.
My sinful life wants to know nothing
    of you.
I doubt in a sense of justice;
the battle robs me of all happiness.
Do I even know if God exists?
Where is then my King and God?

—*Scivias* I, 4, C. 1–7

Abandonment

Who shall comfort me?
For my Mother has abandoned me far
    from the way of salvation.
O Mother Zion, I remember well the joy
    in the house of your glory.
Where shall I flee?

Unspeakable is my pain.
Where are you, O Mother Zion?

I only acknowledged your presence for
    a moment
and hoped for a reunion;
will you abandon me again?
I, the miserable one, strayed from
    your side…
O if only I had never known you,
my pain would be easier to bear.
Weeping and groaning I call to you.
Where does your help for me remain?

—*Scivias* I, 4, C. 1–7

The Painful Pilgrimage

I wander aimlessly in the shadow of death,
a pilgrim in a strange land;
the destination of my travels is my only
    comfort.

I should be a companion of angels, O God,
for I was fashioned from clay by your
    living breath.

But should not I then recognize and
   sense you?

Pain has befallen me,
for the tent of my body turned its eye
   to the north.
Alas, I was held prisoner there
and robbed of my light and the joy
   of wisdom.
My garment was torn apart.
And driven from my inheritance, I was
   led into slavery.

Where am I and how did I get here?
Who will comfort me in my prison?
How can I break these chains?
Who will care for my wounds,
anoint them with oil and show me
   mercy in my pain?

O heaven, hear my cry!
The earth shall tremble with me in
   mourning,
for I am a pilgrim without comfort
   and help.

—*Scivias* I, 4, C. 1–7

Healing
Repentance

Repentance and Reunion

Father, I have sinned against heaven
    and myself,
though you created me as your divine
    work.
Formed and touched by you,
my actions should have been divine.
Because I destroyed the nature of humans
I have also sinned before you.

Self-inflicted misery is my downfall.
I am no longer worthy
of being called your child,
because I have alienated myself
of my own free will
from your creation within me—
the way you have prepared.
Now treat me as your servant,
whose freedom you paid at a high price
in the blood of your Son.

Through Adam the inheritance of your
    children was lost to me.
But now repentance shall repay the
    debt of my sins

with the blood of your Son.

—*Scivias* III, 1, C. 5
(cf. Luke 15:18–19)

Fickleness

O omniscient God, who created
everything good,
I tremble in the knowledge of my sins.
Though I see myself as I am in repentance,
I do not let it move me,
and fear remains my companion.

On the path of willfulness
fear grips me even now in my conceit;
I will become old with my sins.
Although they disgust me, cause me
pain and remorse,
I do not abandon them and I live in fear—
for I know them by number and name.

To the north and east, to the south
and west
the wheel of my life
turns in constant fickleness.

In only one thing does my trust remain:
that you, who have rent the heavens
and clothed yourself in flesh,
will mercifully cleanse me in my penance
and raise me to life.

—LVM Pitra IV, 50 (XXXVIII)

Chastisement

With your scourge, O Lord of the World,
you have chastised me, a sinner,
but you did not laud my torment.

For out of love I searched for you,
confessed to you my sins.
Patiently and wisely I acted,
thus the arbiter of my guilt
knows me as upright.

With both of my wings,
the knowledge of Good and Evil,
I will risk the flight to you
and walk along the path of righteousness.

—LDO I, 2 Migne 774D (XXX)

Lament

O we are but strangers!
What have we done?
We strayed from your way and sinned.
We should be daughters of the King,
but have fallen into the darkness of sin.

O carry us, living Sun,
upon your shoulders to the inheritance
that was once ours and which we lost
through Adam.

O King of Kings,
We fight your battle!

—*Scivias* III, 13, C. 9

Turning Back

I want to turn to the east
and set off on the narrow road.
God, you alone can help me.
I am able to do nothing good without you,

I want to gaze upon you for you give
    me life.
Let your goodness find me.

To you, blessed Virgin, I want to hasten,
to grasp the strong shield of your humility
and join in harmony with the chorus
    of angels:
Glory to you, Oh Lord!

—*Scivias* I, 4, C. 1–7

Healing Wounds

O why am I so downcast,
and bewildered in my soul?
If only for the grace of God
I could wash away
the wounds of sin with my groans
    and tears.
O Lord, through the wounds you suffered
for my sins, inflicted by nail and lance,
I hope for salvation.

—LDO I, 4 Migne 864D (LXXXV)
    (cf. Psalm 41)

The Good Shepherd

O Shepherd of souls,
O first Word, through which we were
    all created,
may it truly please you,
to free us of our misery
and from our brokenness.

—"Song," Nr. 61

Touched by God

What has come over me?
No longer do I know goodness,
nor can I find a path to guide me.

Despair is mine, a sinner. What shall I do?
I do not know, I cannot imagine,
what is to become of me
because of my transgressions.

O where shall I turn,
who will help me
to blot out my shameful sins
and wash them away in contrition?

In my heart I want to turn back,
in true repentance to you, my God,
who has touched my wounds.

Awakened from the sleep of death,
I want to sin no more
in thought, word and deed.

—*Scivias* III, 8, C. 8

Saving Repentance

Why was I born to such great offense?
I have sinned against you in my soul,
    my God.

In my groaning I look up to you,
who deemed it worthy
to take on Adam's form
in the Virgin.

Therefore my trust is steadfast
that you do not despise me,
but will free me from my sins.

Through the holy face of your humanity,
take me up now in your grace,
for I repent with my whole heart.

—LDO I, 4 Migne 830C (XXXII)

Plea for Forgiveness

You, whose power is above all things,
see the blood that was spilled
for all humanity
and forgive us our sins.

We are children of disobedience
and for this we owed you recompense.
But we failed you
because of the transgression in our hearts.

The promise of our baptism we
    did not keep;
we broke your commandments
and threw our innocence away.

But you are loving; do not punish us
as befits our evil,
but release us in your love from
our disobedience.
For have we not, with our whole heart,
forgiven injustice done to us, out of love
and reverence for our Savior?

Have mercy on us, O God,
for you are upright and good!

—*Scivias* II, 8, C. 18
   (cf. Matthew 6:12)

The Blood of Christ

O bloody deed that cried out to heaven,
causing all the elements
to join in lamentation in their distress.
For the blood of their Creator had
   touched them:

O relieve our brokenness!

—"Song," Nr. 77

Prayer for Healing

O where have I come from,
and what am I doing now?
In my lamentation I groan out to you,
   O God,
because I have tainted my understanding
   of you
with the impurity of sin.

Have mercy on me, O Lord,
for I have stained my soul with sin.
Heal the welts of my wounds,
for I have sinned against you.

Teach me more and more my God,
to carry out holy, good deeds,
so that my confused soul
can experience healing through you.

—LDO I, 4 Migne 868D–869A (XC)

Reverence for the Lord

In deep reverence I stand before you,
    O God,
I see my sin as it is,
and I do not evade it.

I groan out to you in love,
and fear your judgment
while rejoicing in your reward.
Although I have not earned
a share in the joys of heaven,
I want to keep myself free of sin.

You give me to eat from the tree of life,
because you find goodness in me,
although the Devil plagues me greatly.

You have laid the fundament of your
    holy works in me,
to take your refuge within.
Let me live in your holy dwelling!

—LVM III, 11 (VIII)

Understanding

Nothing is sweeter for me, O God,
than to hasten to the Creator of the
   universe.
I want to redeem the praises of my mouth
   and heart,
to keep the promises I made to you, my
   upright Judge.

After the acts of wrongdoing
I want to judge myself according to
   your will,
to avoid evil and to do good.

Awareness and understanding burn
   inside me,
with choices made in true obedience.
Because I would rather turn back
to the living God,
than to follow the Devil
in foolish error.

—*Scivias* II, 5, C. 40
   (cf. Psalm 65, 13–14)

Rescue

Lord, may your right hand lift me up,
cleansed of my sin through penance.
Strengthen my longing,
to burn in God's love,
for which my hunger cannot be stilled.

If I arise through repentance,
I will not die in sin,
but snatched from death live forever
to tell of your wondrous deeds.
I will revere and love you,
saved from the corruption of death.

—LDO I, 2 Migne 772A–B (XXVII)
   (cf. Psalm 117)

The Mercy
of God

God's Help

My God, you have created me.
I live through you and strive to do
    your will,
when I beg for goodness in my groaning.

I know you as my God,
blessed in the awareness that I am
    allowed to serve you,
because you have given me
    understanding.

O you, my helper in everything good,
I carry out good works through you.
I want to place all my hopes in you
and put on your garment of favor.

You are my deliverer,
save me from my transgressions
when my conscience warns me
to forsake sin.

—LVM Pitra III, 29 (XXI)
    (cf. Psalm 18:3)

The Way to Light

You have given me two eyes, O God,
to behold in the darkness a glorious light,
to choose the path which I should take.
Whether I be sighted or blind,
I know that I need a guide
throughout the day and into the night.

When I hide in the darkness,
I can then act in malice,
but in the light I will be seen if I do
    the same,
and reap retribution instead of reward.

Living God, I call to you.
Lead me to the way of your light,
and heal my festering sores,
that shame is not mine by day.
Break the bonds of my imprisonment!

—LDO II, 2 Migne 788C (XLV)

Unworthiness

In the deepest part of my soul, Lord,
I see myself as ash and decay.
Like a trembling feather
I sit fearfully in the shadows.

Do not dismiss me like a stranger
from the land of the living.
My reasoning seems foolish
and I take the lowliest place.
I am not worthy to be called human.

O you good and mild Father,
teach me your will!
O Father, worthy of veneration,
do not abandon me
and grant me your mercy!

—*Scivias* III (beginning)

Justice and Mercy

O Lord, I recognize your goodness:
I was not destroyed in spite of my sins,
but you let me retain my freedom.
In the battle against myself I bring forth
    goodness,
while evil brings avarice.

But you always judge in righteousness
and never overstep moderation.
Mercifully you care for me in your
    strength.

And so I humble myself before you
and give honor to your name,
for the sake of your mercy.

—*Scivias* III, 5, C. 11
    (cf. Psalm 119:75)

In the Name of the Church

I was meant to be the bride of your Son,
though I am so weak and fragile.
Heavenly Father I beg you:
Wait no longer with your help!

The limbs of your beloved Son are
    threatened
with division and destruction.
Defend me with all of them,
and direct your merciful gaze toward us.

Turn your face our way,
so that we do not go under!

—LDO III, 10 Migne 1024D (XXII)
    (cf. Psalm 21)

Trusting Despite Misfortune

O, lamentable person that I am,
once a living breath,
I am now surrounded by the stench of sin.
I can no longer look up to heaven in
    happiness.

O where have I come from and
  where am I going?
What good is the righteousness created
  by God if I should go to hell?

But I want to trust in you my Lord,
that I will be freed by true repentance,
from the torment I have brought
  upon myself.
Your grace comforts me and gives
  me strength.

—LDO I, 4 Migne 864C–D (LXXXV)
  (cf. Psalm 41)

Remorse

Father, your child cries out to you,
for your intentions are good
and it knows you as God.

I drink from the dew of your blessings
and smile to you with a remorseful heart.
While in tears I rejoice for your
  name's sake
and call to you: God come to my aid!

With the sound of harps the angels
    answer me,
they praise you when I call.
The dawn of your grace radiates,
and you give to me the bread of life
because I asked for sustenance.

—LVM Pitra IV, 17 (XII)

Hope

O Father of kindness, have mercy
    on the sinners!
You have not abandoned the exiled,
but raised them on your shoulders.
Also we will not perish
because we have set our hopes on you.

—*Scivias* II, 8, C. 6

Liberation

Lord, God, in your merciful grace
rescue me, a sinner, from corruption,
so that I do not deny you with a
    hardened heart.

Rescue me from desires of the flesh,
so through the power of grace,
the fragrance of your good works
may flow from my body.

Rescue me, O God, from my
    impure deeds,
that the thorn of forgetfulness
does not fix me to corruption.

Let me in good conscience
and in the perfume of virtue
trample on iniquity with the feet
of my upright works.

Small are my merits, O God.
Treat me in the way of your goodness.

—LVM Pitra IV, 44 (XXXIII)
    (cf. Psalm 69:15)

Affliction

My God, I call to you
in bitter remorse, with a wounded heart:
heal me, gracious Father,
treat me with mercy in my affliction
for you are my God.

Led by your grace,
I know you in your works.
I seek you in a simple heart
and cry out tearfully for you.

You live in the power of my soul;
the body must atone for my sins.

The eyes of repentance see
the senselessness of my evil deeds.
Receive me now unto you.

—*Scivias* II, 5, C. 54
  (cf. Psalm 55:10)

Redemption

Redeemed by the blood of the Lamb
let us rejoice with our whole heart,
and delight in you with all our soul,
O God of the Trinity, who preserves
    and keeps us.
We want to honor your heavenly reward
for all the suffering and despair
the Enemy of Truth has laid in our path.
But this is of no consequence
when compared with the joy
we savor in your commandments.
Whoever carries out deeds of holiness
embraces you in perfect love.
You give to your beloved all of
    your possessions
and finally the gift of eternal life.

—LDO I, 2 Migne 764D (XIX)
    (cf. Song of Solomon 1)

Godly Life

Living Bread

Who gives you to me—an unhappy
    person in great distress—
in the sweet sacrifice as the Betrothed of
    the Church?
I call you brother, because you have been
    made human.
You drink mercy and truth—the bread
    of humanity—
at the bosom of the Divine.
The Godhead became mother to me,
when it formed and awakened me to life.
The sustenance of the Church is full of
    grace,
for you, the living bread and spring of
    living waters,
promise richness in abundance in the
    sacrament of your body and blood.
For the sake of my redemption you
    became human.
You bless me now with your body
    and blood
that no creature shall despise me.
For you came into this world for my sake

and delivered yourself unto me,
although I rebelled against your com-
    mandments
and proved myself an enemy.

Let me kiss you now, my Brother,
Son of God, and man upon the earth.

—*Scivias* II, 6, C. 35
    (cf. Song of Solomon 8:1)

Father and Son

O you, glorious Father!
We hasten in burning eagerness to you,
we groan to you in loving penance,
our gift received from you.
O Christ, so glorious and exceedingly
    beautiful,
you are the resurrection of life.
Help us remain steadfast,
to rejoice with you.

Never let us be separated from you!

—"Song," Nr. 41

Praise and Petition

Praise be to you, Christ, King of Angels!
Who are you, O God, who placed
this great wisdom, which thwarts the
    Devil's wiles,
in the hearts of publicans and sinners?
They are now radiant in the goodness of
    the Father.

And so praise to you, O King!

O you almighty Father!
A spring flows from you in fiery embers.
Lead your sons over the waters,
with favorable wind for their sails
to the heavenly city of Jerusalem!

—*Scivias* III, 13, C. 9

In the Fire of the Spirit

O fiery Spirit, praise be to you!
You smolder in the hearts of all people and
collect your power in the tabernacles of
    the souls.

Your will arises and fills the souls
    with longing,
that burns with desire like a lamp.

You always wield the sword, cutting off
    the destructive fruit
born of malicious deed, when the fog of
    darkness engulfs our wants and desires.

But the Spirit chastises these wants
    and desires.
It wants to rise up and, looking wickedness
    in the eye, see the malice face to face
and burn it quickly in the fire, according
    to your will.

If reason is forced down into the depths
    of despair by evil deed,
you keep it in check according to your will,
you break it and lead it back through the
    process of the trial.

If wickedness draws its sword against you,
you thrust it back into its own heart,
as you did the first fallen angel
when you cast the tower of his pride
    into hell.

You have built another tower out of tax
    collectors and sinners,
who confess their evil deeds before you.

Thus, all creatures born of you praise you,
for you are the precious ointment
to heal the broken limbs and festering
    wounds
which you transform into precious pearls.

Gather us all to you in your grace and
    lead us on the right path.

Amen.

—"Song," Nr. 18

In the Holy Spirit

O God Almighty,
I dedicate my vows
to your honor.
For, left to my own devices,
I am incapable of anything without you.

Only by the grace of the Holy Spirit
can you be kindled within me.

—LDO I, 4 Migne 854A (LXIX)

Ode to Wisdom

O power of Wisdom,
your influence encircles the universe
leading to the one path of life.

Three powers are yours, like wings they
     serve you:
one soars up to the heavens,
the second circles over the earth
but the third is everywhere.

Wisdom, you are deserving of praise!

—"Song," Nr. 59

Trinitarian Life

Praise be to you, Holy Trinity,
for you are sound and life.

The choirs of angels praise you.
Wonderful, mysterious radiance,
hidden from humankind,
you are life in everything.

—"Song," Nr. 17

Mary

Mary, the New Creation

O sparkling gemstone!
The sun's worthy adornment
poured out in you as a bubbling
    life-spring
from the heart of the Father.
Through his singular Word he created
the unspoiled matter of the earth
    tainted by Eve.

The Father formed the Word in you as a
    human,
and thus you are radiant primary matter,
who received all virtuous powers in a
    single breath,
as every creature is awakened into
    existence.

—"Song," Nr. 5

The Chosen One

O sweet bough full of vigor
on the tree of Jesse,
what great event was this
when the Divine gaze fell upon you,
the most beautiful of women,
as the eagle's eye is fixed upon the sun.
When the Father in heaven saw you,
O Virgin, in your worthiness
and desired to create his Word as flesh
    in you.

Your chaste heart was mystically
    illuminated
through the mystery of God,
and wonderfully a bright flower
sprung from you, O Virgin.

Glory be to God, the Father,
the Son and the Holy Spirit.

—"Song," Nr. 14

The Bearer of God

Hail, Mary,
Author of life,
you have restored deliverance,
conquered death,
and destroyed the serpent which Eve
   raised up,
filled with pride.

You trampled it underfoot as you bore
the Son of God, breathed into you by
   the Holy Spirit.
Hail, sweet loving Mother!
You have born your Son into the world,
sent from heaven
by the breath of God's Holy Spirit.

—"Song," Nr. 3

Our Advocate

O glorious Mother of sacred healing,
through your holy Son
you have poured out oil onto the bitter
   wounds of death,

the torture of the soul passed down
   by Eve.

You have destroyed death
and edified life;
pray for us to your Son,
O Mary Star of the Sea!

O life-giving advocate,
resplendent adornment
and most precious of all joys,
which are never ending in you.

Pray for us, Mary!

—"Song," Nr. 4

Ode to Mary

Hail, greening bough full of vitality!
You came forth into the light
by the flow of the Spirit and the searching
   of the saints.
When the time came you blossomed
   on the bough
and praise was yours.

From you the blazing sun came forth,
like the perfume of balsam.
For the most beautiful of flowers bloomed
     in you,
bestowing fragrance to the withered
     herbs.
They all became resplendent in the
     richest green.

Heaven drenched the grass with dew,
the whole earth became fertile,
giving forth its bounty of wheat,
where the birds of the air built their nests.

Thus, people found their sustenance,
and great was their joy at her table.

Therefore your happiness is never ending,
     O tender Virgin.
All of this was spurned by Eve.

Now praise be to God the Almighty!

—"Song," Nr. 71

Hymn to Mary

Greetings to you, O Virgin!
Generous of heart, glorious and
    immaculate are you,
O orb of chastity
and womb of all holiness.
In this way you were pleasing to God.

For the power of the highest
that clothed the godly Word in flesh
flowed through you.

You, snow-white lily,
whom God looked upon,
above all other creatures.
O most beautiful and pleasing one,
God's greatest delight.
He sowed the embers of his love in you
so that his Son was nourished.

Your being overflowed with joy, O Virgin,
and the symphony of heaven resounded
    in you;
because you bore the Son of God.
your chastity was radiant before the Lord.

Joy then filled your womb
like the grass that drinks the dew,
receiving green vitality.
And so it was with you,
O Mother of every joy.

The whole Church shines with joy
and echoes with harmonious timbre
because of you, O lovely Virgin Mary,
Mother of God who is worthy of praise.
Amen.

—"Song," Nr. 12

Mary, Our Hope

O greening bough,
you stand in your nobleness
and like the dawn you rise.

Rejoice and be happy!
Free us in our weakness
from our evil ways
and offer us your hand
to raise us up from the ground.

—"Song," Nr. 10

Mother of God, Immaculate

O, Bough and Diadem robed in the
    purple of kings,
concealed, you rest as if protected by
    a shield.
You green and bloom in a different way
than Adam, who brought forth the
    human race.

Hail, Mary!
From your womb new life was born,
different from the life Adam robbed from
    his children.

O Flower, not raindrops or dew
have caused you to blossom,
nor did the wind blow above you.
But the glory of God
begot you on the most precious bough.

O Bough, God foresaw your flower
on the first day of creation.
From his Word, O praiseworthy Virgin,
he created the golden primary substance.

How strong and powerful is the side
    of man,
out of which God formed a woman.
He created her as the mirror of his own
    beauty
and the embrace of his entire creation.

Thus, the heavenly harps sound in
    harmony
and all the earth looks on in wonder
at how much God loved you.
Praise to you, Mary!

O, how we lament and mourn
the sad transgression that
came over a woman through the
    serpent's deceit!
Ordained as the mother of creation,
she injured her heart with the wounds
    of ignorance
and brought great suffering to her
    descendants.

But from your womb, O Dawn,
a new sun arose
that blotted out the sins of Eve.

Through you he brought forth greater
blessings
than the affliction caused by Eve to
all people.

And so, O Deliverer, who gave birth
to the new light for the human race,
gather together the members of your Son
in heavenly harmony!

—"Song," Nr. 13

Mary the Prophet

When we, lamentable people,
shamed from generation to generation,
fall down on the path of our pilgrimage,
you call to us with the prophet's voice
and raise us up from the gravest
transgression.

Praise be to you, O Mary!

—"Song," Nr. 9

The Church

Betrothal

O Virgin Church, how painful it was
when your beloved children
were torn from your side,
as if by a wild wolf,
through the deceitful counsel of the
   serpent.

But how precious is the blood of the
   Savior,
who betrothed himself with the Church,
under the victorious banner of the cross,
to win your children back.

—"Song," Nr. 56

Mother Church

Rejoice now, from the depths of your
   heart,
O Mother Church, because your children
are now in holy unity
gathered up in your lap.

But you, O contemptible serpent,
are covered in shame, for the prey
you thought to have devoured
is now radiant in the blood of God's Son.

Praise be to you, O highest King:
Alleluia!

—"Song," Nr. 57

Benevolent Grace

O greatest joy,
that you, my God, work in your way:
bestowing your grace upon the ignorant.
A child does not understand the flight
    of greatness,
but you already gave him his wings.

You treasure those who do not yet know
    themselves,
for their voice cries out to you:
O God, my God, who has created me,
all of my works are yours!

May the Church rejoice in harmony!

—"Song," Nr. 72

Hymn of the Virgin

O tender beloved One who enfolds us,
guard us in our purity.
Sorrow is ours, for we were born
out of the dust of Adam's fall.
And it is a trial for us to resist
the apple's temptation.
Make us your upright people,
O Christ the Savior.

We deeply long to follow you,
but the way is hard for your
    unhappy people
to honorably be like you,
O unblemished and guiltless King
    of Angels.

Yet we trust in you
to seek the precious pearl in the dust.
We call to you as our Bridegroom,
    Comforter
and Savior on the cross.

Like a bride united with you in
    your blood,
we chose you alone as our spouse,
O Son of God.
O Beautiful One, filled with joy and
    precious fragrance,
we groan to you in our lamentable exile.
When shall we see you in this world—
you, who dwell in our soul?
In our hearts we embrace you,
as if we had you here.

O powerful Lion, you tore open the
    heavens
and descended into the lap of the Virgin.
As conqueror of death you gave
to us life in the Golden City.
Let us now live there and
in you, our beloved Spouse.
You have seized us from the grip of
    the Devil,
who led our first parents astray.

—"Song," Nr. 40

The Golden City

Jerusalem, you Golden City,
adorned in the purple of kings!
O edifice of highest goodness,
you are a light that has never dimmed.
You shine in the dawn and in the
    blazing sun.

Your windows, Jerusalem,
are beautifully decorated with topaz
    and sapphire.
Jerusalem, your foundation
is laid with discarded stones
—with the publicans and sinners
who were once lost sheep,
but found by the Son of God
they hastened to you and were placed
    in you.

Thus your walls sparkle with living
    gemstones,
which through the fervor of good will
have soared like clouds up to heaven.
In red-gold, O Jerusalem, your towers
    shimmer and shine,

reflected in your saints and God's
 great glory,
that fills you, O Jerusalem.

O you adorned and crowned people
 of Jerusalem,
the servants of God hasten to help us
as we toil in exile.

—"Song," Nr. 37

The Way and
Aim of Love

The Search for God

I want to revere you, my God and Lord.
Who will help me when I stand before
    you
and free me at your feared judgment seat?
No one, but you alone, my upright God.
I want to seek you and take refuge in you
    until the end of time.

I will not let myself be swayed by my
    wrongful self-will.
I want to turn back to you, my Father,
who did not give in to the wiles of the
    Devil.
I want to believe in you, my Lord, One
    God in Three Persons,
to glorify and honor you and to place my
    trust in you.

I carry your name in my heart for all
    eternity.

—*Scivias* II, 8, C. 3–5

Longing

My home is in heaven,
where I meet all your creation,
God's love is my desire,
and to raise up the tower of longing,
    my wish.

I want to do what you ask of me, O God.
On wings of good will
I fly above the stars in heaven
to do your will.

Nothing else remains for me to search
    or wish for,
I long only for holiness.

Let me, O God, be your harp and zither
    of love!

—LVM Pitra IV, 15 (X)

Godly Commandments

In flesh that does not consent to goodness,
I long for you and receive you.
O Lord, in my heart of hearts,
I contemplate your laws
against the will of my flesh.

As the mill grinds grain
for nourishment with the help of water,
I want to plumb and eagerly fulfill
all of your commandments in the midst
    of the torrent
of my weak human nature.

—LDO I,4 Migne 864A–B (LXXXIV)

Obedience

In harmony with the promise of
    your Word,
I ring out like a zither.
Only what comes from you, O God,
do I want to sense, take pleasure in,
    and aspire to.
For I emanated from you,

have been nurtured by you,
and desire no other God but you.
My obedience to you sustains me.

—LVM Pitra III, 14 (X)

Under God's Protection

O God, you defend those who believe
    in you.
Keep me safe in your omnipotence.
I find shelter under your wings,
and honor you in thanksgiving and
    praise.
Never do I lift my eyes to a God who
    disappoints me
and does not know me.

Free me from the tormenting spirits of evil
that arise in desires of the flesh
and grant me perfect victory.
My soul rejoices in my body
because it obtains for her eternal reward.

—LDO I, 4 Migne 818A–B (XX)
    (cf. Psalm 16)

The Saving Name

Almighty Father,
we call on you now in our great need.
We entreat you through your Word,
which grants us in plenty what we need
    for life.
Look upon us now, Father,
as is fitting to your name, and help us,
so we do not perish and your name
    darken within us.
May it be worthy of you to come to
    our aid
through this your holy name!

—"Song," Nr. 1

Faithful Petition

I believe in you, O God, in true devotion,
and fulfill your works in faith.
Multiply happiness in each of these
    virtues,
O Lord of the World, my greatest joy!

I want to follow you in faith and love,
because you are my Creator.

You give me what is good;
I do not lack what I ask for and desire.
Faith shall teach me the rightful petition:
Give me only what is pleasing to you
and everlasting.

When I groan to you in need
for my brother or myself,
let me attain your love through holy,
    good works.
Fulfill my upright wishes!

—LVM Pitra V, 62 (XLVI)
    (cf. Psalm 36:4)

Triumphant in God

My Creator and Lord, you are my
    strength.
Without you I can do no good,
for I live through your Spirit.
It is what stirs me and reveals my way
    to me.

I want to call on you God and Lord,
let me walk the way of your laws,
as the deer hastens to the spring.

Lead me beyond earthly desire
to the summit of power and victory.
Having reached divine salvation,
I want to tirelessly sing your praises.

—LDO I, 3 Migne 796B–C (V)
   (cf. Habakkuk 3)

True Reverence and Love

O Lord, we call you Lord in the name
   of reverence,
and for the sake of love we call you God.
You are named Almighty
because you encircle everything in
   your power.

Your way of justice is upright and true,
for all fears are destroyed through
   genuine reverence of you,
and every love is united with the true
   love to you.

All forces are ruled by your power.
I know that I can do nothing without you,
and find in you my comfort.

—LVM Pitra I, 57 (XLIV)
   (cf. Revelation 16:7)

True Faith

Inspired by the counsel of the Holy Spirit,
we want to draw near to the greatest joy
   with an upright mind,
to begin what is good with a peaceful
   heart
and to consummate it in devotion.

Brotherly love is kindled by peace;
it follows the example of your goodness,
   O God,
and encompasses the needs of all people.
So bring our heart, simple and pure,
to fulfillment in true faith.

—LVM Pitra III, 49 (XL)

Fulfilled in Your Way

I am enthroned above the stars
because your gifts suffice me.
Trusting in you, I delight in the sweet
    sound of the timpani.

I kiss the sun and embrace the moon,
    holding it tightly;
the fruits of their labor suffice me.
What more should I wish for,
what more could I need?

Everything is proof of your loving mercy.
I may live in the house of the King and
    sit at his table,
for I am a daughter of the King.

—LVM Pitra V,13 (IX)

From Virtue to Virtue

I followed you faithfully, O Son of God,
along the path of your truth.
Through your humanity you redeemed
    the human race.

O Navigator of the universe, convey me
to the bounty of your gifts,
which I proceed toward with confidence—
fortified by your strength—from virtue
    to virtue.

Thus on the right path,
I abandon myself and savor your virtues:
Drinking of them I am strengthened.

The righteous one, whom God so loves,
will sense no weariness but lasting
    salvation.

—LDO I, 2, 19 Migne 764C–765B

Love

Teach me with the breath of the Holy
    Spirit
that pure water flows from me,
tears stream from the groan of longing
    for good deeds,
and sweet perfume wafts from holy works.
By day I want to act on the virtue of
    serenity
and anoint the night of all pain.

—LVM Pitra III, 8 (VI)

Holiness

I call to you, O God: give me what I
    need for life!
You have good plans for me, I may
    see you and know you.

My virtuous conscience senses you,
    my God.

I strike the zither of prayer when I
      experience you in worship.
Girded with temperance I blossom in joy.

Consummate, O God, your works
through the heavenly hosts of Christ
      the King
who I lead into battle.

—LVM Pitra IV, 9 (VI)

Glorification

Let us praise the Lord, our God,
For we have been glorified in him,
and have won the victory in his name.

Our strength lifts him up to praise.
Let us carry forth the triumph
over his enemies and ours,
because we are loyal to him
and our faithfulness to him is constant.

—LDO III, 10 Migne 1026A (XXIV)

Salvation

I call to you, O my God, and you
    answer me.
I ask you for help and your goodness
    gives me what I long for;
in you I find what I seek.

Filled with reverence and joy,
I strike the zither before you, my God,
for all of my deeds are done in
    your name.
I set all of my hopes on you
and rest peacefully in your bosom.

—LVM Pitra II, 19 (XII)

Life after Death

I want to have a happy life
in the peace of eternity.
In the days when life blossoms in fullness
and I grow and mature in holiness,
I want to honor my Creator
in good and holy works.

There comes the time when flesh and
    blood
fall away from the bone.
The ash of the body
becomes the dust of the earth from which
    I was formed
and enters another life.

The spirit quickening my body
leaves it and returns
to the Lord of Creation,
who gave to me my body
by the power of his grace.

O Creator, you are like a blacksmith
who flames the fire with his billows,
examines his work from every side
and brings it to completion.

When I have found the way home
to eternal joy,
conveyed by good deeds,
let me see the purest light.

Let me hear the song of the angels
and joyfully receive again

the garment of my body,
which I have taken off.

—LVM IV, 68 (LIII)
   (cf. Ecclesiastes 12:1)

The Way and Aim of Love

Teach me, O God, in the Holy Spirit
to follow your way,
to receive the bread of life
that you give to your chosen and
   sanctified.

Take me up in the highest joy
of your goodness and
let me rest in your bosom.

—LVM Pitra III, 29 (XXI)
   (cf. Psalm 18:3)

In the Light of the Angel Choir

O you glorious angels of living light!
In the deep mystery of your being,
each of you at the throne of the Godhead
looks with burning desire into the eyes
    of God;
never can your gaze be satiated.
What glorious joy lies hidden in your
    nature,
untouched by that first terrible act
committed by a member of your legion—
the angel who fell.
He wanted to fly over the battlements
concealed in the heart of God;
agonized and broken, he sank in
    the rubble.
With devious counsel he lent the
    instrument of his fall
to the creature made by the hand of God.

But you, O angels, protectors of all people,
whose nature reflects your glorious face,
O Archangels, who receive the
    righteous souls,

your powers, forces and principalities,
your sovereignties and your thrones
are united in the five mysteries.
O Cherubim and Seraphim,
seal upon the mystery of God,
you are worthy of praise!
You gaze in peace on the source of the
    eternal heart
and see face to face the heart of the Father
breathing out his inner power.

—"Song," Nrs. 20, 21

The Prayer of Christ
(*Ordo Viritutum*, Epilogue)

In the beginning all creation awakened
    to life in green vitality,
the flowers bloomed in the middle of time;
but then the vitality dried to dust.

Look to me now, my Father,
in whom you are reflected.
Exhaustion has overcome my body;

my children yield to human weakness.
O Father, consider that the hope of
    the beginning
should not have withered away
until the golden sum of your numbers
    has been filled!

At that time it was never your intention
to turn your eyes away,
before you gazed upon my body
adorned with precious jewels.

I succumb to weariness
for the sake of my scorned members.
Father, look at me,
for I show you my wounds!

Pain overcomes me, for my members
have turned away from me
and heed the Son of Corruption.
Yet I bring home again
those who have fallen among them.

Father, I am your Son!
Look upon me with the love
you gave me to bring forth into the world.

Gaze upon the wounds
through which I granted salvation
    to humanity
according to your will.
Have mercy on your people
and do not let their names be erased
from your Book of Life.

Through the blood of my wounds
carry them back in repentance to you.

All you daughters and sons,
    bend your knees
before your Father, so he can
reach out his loving hand to you.

—LDO III, 10 Migne 1034C (XXXIV)

Sources

Critical Edition, in *Corpus Christianorum Continuatio Mediaevalis,* Vol. 43, 43A, Adelgundis Führkötter, o.s.b., and Angela Carlevaris, o.s.b., eds., Turnholti, Belgium: Brepols, 1978.

Hildegard of Bingen, Songs, based on the manuscripts of Pudentiana Barth, o.s.b., Maria-Immaculata Ritscher, o.s.b., and Joseph Schmidt-Görg, Salzburg, 1969.

Ordo Viritutum (*Play of the Virtues*), published by the Abbey of St. Hildegard in Eibingen as *Ordo Viritutum: Reigen der Tugenden* (*Round Dance of the Virtues*), Berlin, 1927.

Patrologia Latina, Vol. 197, J. P. Migne, ed.,
  Paris, 1882.

Sanctae Hildegardis Opera. Analecta Sacra,
  Vol. 8, J. B. Pitra, ed., Monte Cassino,
  1882.

Scivias, Walburga Storch, O.S.B., ed., trans.,
  Augsburg, 1990.

To learn more about
HILDEGARD OF BINGEN

ST. HILDEGARD ABBEY in Rüdensheim/ Eibingen, Germany, maintains an excellent Web site in German only, at present: **www.abstei-st-hildegard.de**. The site offers a history of the abbey and information about the daily life, work and community of Benedictine sisters there. Visitors to the site can take two interactive tours through the abbey and cloister church. Information is also available for those who wish to visit the abbey, or spend time there in spiritual retreat.